THE HOME FRONT

EVACUATION

Fiona Reynoldson

THE HOME FRONT

THE BLITZ
EVACUATION
PRISONERS OF WAR
PROPAGANDA
RATIONING
WOMEN'S WAR

Editor: Catherine Ellis
Series designer: Nick Cannan
Consultant: Terry Charman, researcher and historian at the Imperial War Museum

First published in 1990 by
Wayland (Publishers) Limited
61 Western Road, Hove
East Sussex BN3 1JD

British Library Cataloguing in Publication Data
Reynoldson, Fiona
Evacuation.
1. Great Britain. Children. Evacuation, 1939-1945
I. Title II. Series
940.5361610941

HARDBACK ISBN 1-85210-873-8

PAPERBACK ISBN 0-7502-0948-8

Typeset by Rachel Gibbs, Wayland
Printed and bound by Casterman S.A., Belgium

CONTENTS

The Threat of War

The First World War was the first time that aeroplanes were ever used to drop bombs. Using aeroplanes, bombs could be dropped on the enemy's towns and factories as well as on battlefields. After the First World War people began to worry about what would happen if there was another war. What if bombs with explosives or poison gas were dropped on Britain's cities? It was a frightening idea:

'. . . it is possible . . . that the amount of explosives dropped from aeroplanes might exceed in the first twenty-four hours (of the next war) the whole weight of explosives dropped in the whole of the period of the last war.' (Minutes of the Subcommittee on Air Raid Precautions, 1924.)

No one knew how to defend Britain from air attacks. France was only twenty-two miles across the Channel, and London was only about seventy miles from the coast. Planes could fly from the north coast of France and Belgium and bomb London. It was not the same for

German cities were deep in the heart of Europe. British cities were easier for German planes to reach.

Left *Many German people supported Hitler because he was a strong leader who would make Germany rich and powerful again. They did not see the dangers. These soldiers are Hitler's own storm troopers – the Sturmabteilung (SA), or Brownshirts as they were often called.*

Below *Before long signposts were removed so that if the Germans invaded they would not know where they were.*

Germany. In the 1920s and 1930s hardly any British bombers could fly far enough to reach the big German cities.

Adolf Hitler became the leader of Germany in 1933. It was obvious that he wanted to make Germany powerful again. In Britain many people were alarmed by Hitler and his growing armies.

'There is no doubt that the Germans are already stronger than us in the air and they are manufacturing at such an alarming rate that we cannot catch them up.' (Letter from Winston Churchill to his wife, 1933.)

During the 1930s some people in Britain began to plan how to evacuate (get people out of) Britain's cities in case there was a war.

Britain's Evacuation Plans

Above *A government poster.*

London was by far the largest city in Britain. The London County Council made detailed plans to evacuate the city. It divided London into six areas. Each area was based around one or two big London stations, from which children were sent on trains into the country.

The whole country was divided into areas: evacuation areas, neutral areas and reception areas. The idea was to move children over five years of age, pregnant mothers, mothers with children under five and disabled people away from evacuation areas such as London. They would be safe, big cities would have fewer mouths to feed and fewer injured and dead to deal with in the terrible bombing that was expected.

Right *Children sheltering in a trench in Kent during the Battle of Britain. It was the fear of air attack that made so many mothers agree to evacuation.*

Reception areas were safe country areas, far away from the cities:

'We were living in Ilford and my sisters and I were sent to Ipswich.' (Kate Taylor, Ilford.)

'I was evacuated from Birmingham to near Bristol. I and five other boys were sent to the country estate of the Fry family – the chocolate people. We lived there helping on the farm for the rest of the war.' (Dennis Baker, Birmingham.)

No one had to be evacuated, but all mothers were told it was for the best. Some cities were very keen on evacuation and were very well organized. 75 per cent of children were evacuated from Manchester. Only 15 per cent were evacuated from Sheffield.

The Government moved one-and-a-half million people in a week. At the same time, two million people arranged their own, or their children's evacuation. This was the largest mass movement of people ever seen in Britain.

'We didn't lose one single child or have one accident.' (Hugh Eller, London County Council Evacuation Area Organizer.)

Escape to Safety

The Second World War started in September 1939. Not only Britain had thought about evacuation. France and Germany had also made plans.

In Germany, people who lived in an area near the French border called the Saar-Phalz were evacuated soon after war was declared. More than half a million Germans were moved to safer areas, away from where there might be fighting.

The French also worried about their border with Germany. They built a huge line of forts called the Maginot Line to protect the border. When war broke out, the French evacuated everyone who lived around the Maginot Line. Altogether about half a million people left Strasbourg and all the nearby towns and villages.

'I visited Strasbourg while I was at the Front. It is a city of death. Most of the shops have their shutters up, but some had none to put up . . . At a pastry cook's, little cakes and sweets lie mouldering in the window. Things had to be left as they were while the owners huddled a few clothes into a bag . . .' (*France at War*, Somerset Maugham.)

Above *Refugees in Britain. Many people, particularly Jews, fled from Nazi Germany.*

Right *Civilians being evacuated by the German Army in 1940–41. All over Europe fear of bombing or the needs of the armies forced people to move.*

The evacuees went by slow open trains hundreds of miles to the south-west of France. Every day 10,000 or more arrived, exhausted and homeless. It was a terrible job finding places for them to sleep – in houses, barns and cowsheds.

In May and June 1940 the German Army went round the Maginot Line and advanced towards Paris. The Parisians had no time to think about evacuation plans. They just fled in cars, taxis or on foot, or they stayed to face the Germans.

In 1940 French roads were jammed with evacuees fleeing before the German advance.

Getting Ready to Go

Above *A child at school waiting to be evacuated. The belongings he was going to take with him are on his table.*

The British Government gave out a leaflet called *Evacuation Why and How?*, telling parents all about evacuation and who was to go. Those who stayed in the cities were there to keep the factories, offices, hospitals and shops going.

The areas to be evacuated under the Government scheme were:

'(**a**) London, as well as West Ham and East Ham; Walthamstow, Leyton, Ilford and Barking in Essex; Tottenham, Hornsey, Willesden, Acton and Edmonton in Middlesex; (**b**) the Medway towns of Chatham, Gillingham and Rochester; (**c**) Portsmouth,

Right *What you could take if you were evacuated.*

Evacuees in Gravesend, Kent. Notice that all of them are carrying gas masks in boxes, and that each child is wearing a label.

Gosport and Southampton; (**d**) Birmingham and Smethwick; (**e**) Liverpool, Bootle, Birkenhead and Wallasey; (**f**) Manchester and Salford; (**g**) Sheffield, Leeds, Bradford and Hull; (**h**) Newcastle and Gateshead; (**i**) Edinburgh, Rosyth, Glasgow, Clydebank and Dundee.' (*Evacuation Why and How?*)

In all these places local Councils organized trains and timetables. Headmasters made lists of those children who were being evacuated. Teachers were told to be ready to go. Mothers packed cases for their children.

'We went to school every day with sandwiches, gas masks and great big labels. And every day we came back from school again. We didn't know which day we were being evacuated.' (Gerald Moss, from *No Time to Wave Goodbye*, Ben Wicks.)

Parents were given a list of what to pack for their children. Some families were very poor and could not provide all the clothes on the list.

'We marched through the streets of Wandsworth just as we'd done several times before, heading for the railway station. Only this time people stood on their doorsteps to watch us pass and shopkeepers gave us sweets and packets of nuts and raisins.' (Michael Aspel, from *The Evacuees*, B.S. Johnson.)

Saying Goodbye

A million or more mothers and fathers had to say goodbye to their children in playgrounds, at school gates and at railway stations all over the country. If the bombing was as bad as was expected they might never see them again.

'I thought it was a Sunday School outing down to the seaside. And I looked out of the bus window and I saw my mother crying outside and I said to my brother, "What's Mummy crying for?" and my brother said: "Shut up!" ' (Alan Burrell, from *No Time to Wave Goodbye*.)

'My dad suddenly vanished, he left us in the middle of the school yard. He couldn't bear to be in the hall of the school with us, so he just walked away so he wouldn't break down and cry in front of us.' (David Gurr, from *No Time to Wave Goodbye*.)

Evacuees could be spotted easily by the labels on their coats, the bags in their hands, and their gas masks:

Brighton station September 1939. Many parents accompanied children to relatives in the country and then had to say goodbye to them and go back to London.

A few months after the evacuation of 1939, Germany defeated France. The Nazis were now just across the Channel. This set off an invasion scare, and towns on the southern coast of Britain were urged to evacuate their children.

Pupils from Hugh Myddleton School in London, ready to be evacuated.

'We all had black ones except my little sister. She had a red one with a red nose on it that flapped up and down.' (Jean Carberry, from *No Time to Wave Goodbye*.)

At the beginning of the war everyone had to carry their gas masks around with them. The government was afraid that German planes would drop gas bombs on cities. Gas masks were uncomfortable to wear. Patricia Ferman remembered:

'. . . the awful choking sensation and sweating inside that rubber mask . . . although I remember taking it on the train and being made aware that it was my most valuable possession, never to be out of sight, I don't recall ever using or seeing it again.' (*No Time to Wave Goodbye*.)

The Journey and Arrival

Schoolboys leaving London. Thousands of teachers went with them. This meant closing schools in London and finding buildings to use as schools in the country.

Thousands of children travelled all day on trains. They did not know where they were going. Often there were no corridors in the trains, so no way of getting to the toilet. By evening they were tired and hungry. Some had been sick. Some had soiled their pants. The journey no longer seemed like an outing or a holiday. They tumbled out of the trains in the dark to spend the night with people they had never seen before.

'I remember the arrival of the "vackies" as we nicknamed them. I was a cub and the Patrol Leader told us that evacuees from Liverpool and Manchester were arriving on Saturday and we were to help. Trainloads kept arriving. They were taken to Station Road Chapel. Hot drinks, sandwiches, biscuits etc. were handed out and each child was carrying their sole possessions in a suitcase or parcel, gas mask and identity-tag [label]. Some children treated it as a great adventure, others quietly sobbed. (Boy aged ten, from *Children of the Blitz*, Robert Westall.)

'The foster mothers . . . just walked about the field picking out what they considered to be the most presentable specimens and then harassed the poor billeting officers for the registration slips which were essential if they were to get the cash for food and lodging from the government.' (Susan Waters, infant teacher, from the Mass-Observation Archive.)

Billeting officers were people in the reception areas. Their job was to find 'billets', or foster homes, for all the evacuated children, teachers and mothers with children.

Foster parents were paid 10s 6d (52½p) for one child, and 8s 6d (42½p) for each additional child they took in.

Above Billeting officers and education officers checking on pupil numbers at Kingsbridge Station in Devon. A train had just arrived with 174 pupils from Bristol.

Below An advertisement aimed at foster parents.

Being Chosen

There is one memory that stays with most evacuees. That is the moment of being chosen by foster parents. Often this took place in a village hall, late at night, after a long day's travelling.

> 'We felt like cattle at an auction when one of the remaining ladies declared: "All right I'll take these two." ' (*No Time to Wave Goodbye.*)
>
> 'My mother had said that I must stay with my younger brother and sister. On no account was I to leave them. We sat in the village hall and it got darker and darker. People came in and picked other children all around us. But nobody wanted the three of us.' (Jane Clarke, Manchester.)
>
> 'If you were a child with glasses or with spots you were always left till the end.' (Joan Topp, from *No Time to Wave Goodbye.*)

Evacuees from West Ham waiting to be billeted in foster homes in Cornwall.

Left Children arriving at their foster parents' home.

Some children didn't get chosen at all. The billeting officer drove them from house to house or walked the streets knocking on doors, asking people to take the last of the children in for the night at least.

Some children walked back to London, or at least they set out.

'Micky and I walked home with the odd lift we thumbed. My mum opened the door and nearly fainted. "What you doin' here," she said. "Your Dad'll kill you!" ' (Jim Willis, London.)

Many children did not stay long anyway. The weeks passed and no bombs fell on the big cities. The children went home. Not only had many children desperately missed their homes and families, many parents hated being separated too.

By Christmas 1939 nearly half the schoolchildren who had been evacuated had gone home.

Below This advertisement tried to encourage more people to take in evacuees. It was a hard job to find enough foster parents.

Thank you, Foster-Parents . . . we want more like you!

Some kindly folk have been looking after children from the cities for over six months. Extra work? Yes, they've been a handful! . . . but the foster-parents know they have done the right thing.

And think of all the people who have cause to be thanking the foster-parents. First, the children themselves. They're out of a danger-zone — where desperate peril may come at any minute. And they're healthier and happier. Perhaps they don't say it but they certainly mean "Thank you".

Then their parents. Think what it means to them!

The Government are grateful to all the 20,000 people in Scotland who are so greatly helping the country by looking after evacuated children. But many new volunteers are needed—to share in the present task and to be ready for any crisis that may come. Won't you be one of them? All you need do is enrol your name with the local Authority. You will be doing a real service for the nation. You may be saving a child's life.

The Secretary of State, who has been entrusted by the Government with the conduct of evacuation, asks you urgently to join the Roll of those who are willing to receive children. Please apply to your local Council.

Different Homes

Evacuees found themselves in all sorts of different homes. Sometimes children came up against hatreds that they didn't know existed. Abigail Sabel was a Jewish child from London, evacuated to Berkshire.

'Every Sunday we were asked if we would like to go with them to church and we said no. Eventually the woman insisted and my sister told her we went to a synagogue [a Jewish temple], not a church. She was absolutely horrified. She said to us, get out! In the East End no one had ever said anything like that.' (*A People's War*, Peter Lewis.)

Boys helping on a farm. Many evacuees loved their taste of life in the country.

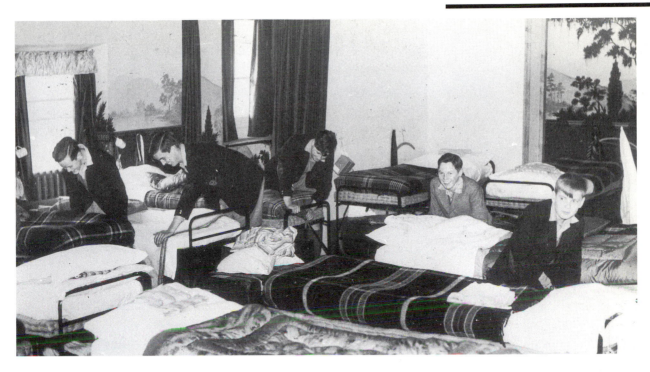

Luck and the child's temperament played the biggest part in whether an evacuee was happy or not. Some had terrible experiences. Some found a new marvellous life and love in the homes of their foster parents.

'I found myself billeted with an old farming couple . . . in North Pembrokeshire. Here was a new world of woods, green fields and strange, dark men speaking Welsh. This was a far cry from the Blitz-battered debris of Swansea. There I had shared a bed with my two brothers, gone shoeless and lived on dry toast and dripping. This was another life – fresh country food, a room of my own . . .' (Bryn Griffiths, from *The Evacuees*.)

Children were sent to aunts, uncles, grandparents and friends. John Moore was six years old when he was taken from Coventry to an evacuated boarding school in Wales. At first most pupils were upset at being left:

'But boys, like puppies, are usually pretty adaptable. One or two ran away and did not return; . . . I had the good fortune to make good friends and I found that after two or three weeks the homesickness abated.' (John Moore, Coventry.)

Above *These schoolboys were evacuated to a Cumberland hotel. They are making up beds in the dining room.*

Below *Evacuated children in Hertfordshire, September 1939.*

Homesickness

Many children were very homesick and frightened. Bedwetting was a serious problem. Many people did not realize that the evacuees who wet their beds were not dirty. The bedwetting was a sign of being unhappy.

'I was an only child and we had an evacuee to stay. Everyone said how good it would be for me to have a brother. I thought he was horrid and he wet the bed.' (Val Collins, Surrey.)

Sometimes no one understood or wanted the children at all:

'Clarence and I used to sleep together and poor Clarence used to wet the bed, 'cause he was a very nervous kid. She [the foster mother] could never tell

Below *This government poster tried to persuade mothers not to bring their children back to the cities.* Below right *These evacuees came from the East End of London. Life in the country was very different to what they were used to.*

who'd done it so she used to bash the daylights out of the both of us. So, of course, the more Clarence got hit the more he wet the bed. It was then we started to get locked in the cupboard.' (Michael Caine, from *No Time to Wave Goodbye*.)

Sponged mattresses and bedding hung out to dry were common sights in the kindest households. And although many evacuees came from good homes, many came from city slums. They arrived in middle-class homes in the country. The shock to both sides was enormous.

'Evacuation took place at the end of a long summer holiday, when schools had not held their de-lousing parades for a long time. In some places people estimated as many as half the evacuees were verminous. Some children had never worn night clothes and some had no change of underwear.' (*A Peoples' War*.)
'Some children (from Manchester) had never slept in beds. One boy had never had a bath.' (*Town Children Through Country Eyes*, a Women's Institute Report.)

Excited children greeting their parents. Travelling was difficult in the war. Few people owned cars and petrol was rationed. Train travel was expensive and often disrupted. Fathers might be away fighting or, like mothers, working long hours in factories, so visits to evacuated children were rare.

Mothers and Children

Mothers and children at Marylebone Station, London, waiting to leave for the North of England.

Children who were under five were evacuated with their mothers, if their mother wanted to go. Some women did not want to leave their husbands. But many women were on their own with children anyway, as their husbands were in the army, navy or air force.

'My father joined the air force and moved around. My mother rented a small flat near her parents and we stayed there for the whole of the war.' (Jack Barker, London.)

Not everyone could be so independent. Many women left London and the other cities in trains just like the schoolchildren.

'I went with Brian, who was three and left Ted, my husband. He wanted me to be safely out of the way. He was doing some sort of war work I think. I finished up at a cottage in Hertfordshire and stayed there a long time. We got on beautifully with our hosts, sharing a kitchen and all that, and we're still in touch now, all these years later.' (Lil Lawrence, Kent.)

Many mothers who were evacuated found country life dull and quiet. They missed the buzz of living in a city, and entertainments like the cinema.

Not every evacuated mother fitted in so well. Town and country people were very different. Many country women were horrified at having to share their homes and kitchens:

> 'They found it hard to be sympathetic to women who could neither cook nor sew, and whose idea of enjoyment was to visit the public house or cinema.' (Women's Institute Report.)

Many townswomen, on the other hand, found country life so boring and quiet that they longed to be back home.

> 'She was nice enough when she came to stay with us, but quiet and depressed all the time she was with us. "Bombs or no bombs," she said, "I'm going home!" ' (May Savage, Cheshire.)

Serious bombing did not take place until September 1940. When it did come it was terrible, but many people did not want to leave their homes, despite the danger.

Evacuation Overseas

When war began some people decided that even the countryside wasn't safe enough. They wanted to send their children overseas to places like Canada, the USA, Australia and South Africa.

'My father was determined I should go to American friends. I had a jolly good six years. I found myself miles ahead of the American schoolchildren, so life was easy.' (J.M. Turner, Kent.)

Some did not find it so easy:

'My first memory of Canada is a huge dark room. My father, like everyone else in England, was not allowed to buy dollars; he was unable to supply us with any money at all. So my mother depended on Canadian friends to clothe and feed us for four years.' (Elizabether Forsyth, from *The Evacuees*.)

British evacuees going to South Africa.

The Cuthbert children enjoyed their evacuation to their aunts in Australia much more:

'On the morning of departure buses took us down to Liverpool docks. We had to wait hours – then we were aboard our home for the next eleven weeks. It was a Polish ship, a former luxury liner. The crew took us to their hearts and were kindness itself. I think the first week must have been trying for everyone. We were chased by submarines, although heavily escorted by other ships: there was great homesickness and much seasickness, lifeboat drill and lots of singing.' (H. Cuthbert, from *The Evacuees*.)

The sisters recall five very happy years in Australia.

Perhaps more children would have been sent abroad, but then on 17 September 1940 the Germans sank an evacuee ship on its way to Canada. Most parents decided to keep their children in Britain from then on.

LEAVE THIS TO US SONNY — <u>YOU</u> OUGHT TO BE OUT OF LONDON

MINISTRY OF HEALTH EVACUATION SCHEME

British poster from 1942.

Children being given medical examinations by women doctors before being evacuated overseas.

Evacuation Again

As the months went by, more and more evacuees drifted home because no bombs had fallen. But it was the lull before the storm.

In June 1940, France fell to the Germans. The British Army was rescued from Dunkirk in northern France. Suddenly the Germans were just across the English Channel. Many people were afraid that England would be invaded. Evacuation schemes started all over again.

Fear of this sort of bomb damage made some parents send their children away to safety.

In 1940 the British were very afraid of a German invasion. The south coast was fringed with miles of barbed wire. Children who had been evacuated from the cities to the coast, were moved again.

'I was at St. Joseph's College as a boarder. My mother appeared one day insisting that she was evacuating me to the country that day. The headmaster was very angry, saying the school was being evacuated in two weeks. My mother insisted it had to be that day. Later it transpired that my father, who worked for the Intelligence Services, had had some sort of warning that the Germans were about to invade!' (Michael Sheard, Surrey.)

Children were evacuated from towns on the South Coast of England in case the Germans invaded.

'In 1939 I was evacuated to Eastbourne, where I was quite happy and getting on well at school. Then in 1940 I was evacuated again. This time to Wales.' (Phyllis Bates, London.)

The Battle of Britain raged over the South of England in July and August 1940. Then came the Blitz. London was bombed night after night. This was what everyone had feared would happen. The other major cities were bombed too. Children were evacuated again but not as many as before.

In 1944 and 1945 Germany began to bomb Britain with the V-1 (a pilotless 'flying bomb') and the V-2 (a rocket). These caused such destruction around London that once again a few children were evacuated.

A V-2 rocket. Between October 1944 and May 1945 1,000 V-2s landed in Britain, half of them in London.

German Evacuation 1945

Germans on their way to surrender in May 1945. The war had caused millions of people to leave their homes. The end of the war saw more disruption. In a war-torn Europe, sixteen million East Europeans became refugees. Two million died.

In June 1944 the British and Americans invaded northern France and began to push the German forces back. By the end of 1945 the Russians were poised to invade Germany from the east. To try to save some of its people from the Russian advance, Germany decided to evacuate people from the east.

'It was 26 January 1945. The city of Gdynia on the Gulf of Danzig was hidden under clouds of snow. Women muffled up to their eyes were going with their children from door to door to beg for a cup of warm milk. There

A German evacuee convoy in the Baltic Sea, 1945.

were children too, who pulled their sick mothers along on sleighs or boards searching for a doctor, a bed or just a warm corner.' (*Flight in the Winter*, Juergen Thorwald.)

Millions of panic-stricken refugees poured into the German-held ports on the Baltic Sea. Ambulance trains arrived loaded with German soldiers wounded in battles with the Russians.

'For all, the unthinkable fate was to fall into the hands of the Russians; and for all there was only one practical way of escape. That was by sea.' (*The Cruellest Night*, Christopher Dobson, John Miller and Ronald Payne.)

The Wilhelm Gustloff was a big ship. Normally it carried 1,900 people. On the night of 30 January 1945, 8,000 people crowded on board – refugees, soldiers and wounded soldiers. Tragically, a Russian submarine spotted the ship making its way through the choppy, ice-cold sea. The Wilhelm Gustloff was torpedoed and sunk. Five times more people died than on the Titanic.

But the evacuation went on. Over two million refugees and soldiers were evacuated on every kind of ship, from liners to trawlers, between 23 January and 8 May 1945. Then the war in Europe ended.

A German painting showing civilians being evacuated after an air raid on Berlin.

GLOSSARY

Auction   Sale where people buy by bidding.

Billeting officers   People who arranged homes and foster parents for evacuees.

Billets   Homes to which evacuees were sent to live.

East End   The east side of London.

Evacuate   Get people out of a place.

Evacuation areas   Places most likely to be bombed (dangerous).

Foster parents   People who had evacuees to stay.

Front, the   Where the fighting is in a war.

Neutral areas   Places fairly unlikely to be bombed.

Presentable specimens   Best-looking children.

Reception areas   Places very unlikely to be bombed (safe).

Refugee   Someone who has to leave their home (often because of fighting) and who is trying to find a safe place.

Registration slips   Pieces of paper to say a child was going to stay with a foster parent.

Synagogue   Jewish temple.

Torpedoed   Blown up by torpedoes (under-water bombs).

Transpired   Came to be known.

Verminous   Having vermin (usually lice) on the body and head.

PROJECTS

1   It is 1939. Imagine you are going to be evacuated with your school. Make a list of all the things you would take with you. Remember you have only a small suitcase or large paper carrier bag.

2   Interview relatives and friends who were evacuated in 1939. Ask questions like: Did you go with your school? Where did you go to? Who did you stay with? Was it very different from your home? How long did you stay there?

3   Imagine you have an evacuee staying with you. Write about what it is like to have someone else in your house, from your point of view. Then try to imagine what the evacuee must have felt far from home. Write a paragraph about what he or she must have felt.

BOOKS TO READ

Books for younger readers

Nance Lui Fyson, *Growing up in the Second World War* (Batsford, 1981)

Madeline Jones, *Life in Britain in World War II* (Batsford, 1983)

Kathleen Monham, *Growing up in World War II* (Wayland, 1979)

Miriam Moss, *How They Lived – A Schoolchild in World War II* (Wayland, 1988)

Fiona Reynoldson, *War at Home* (Heinemann Educ., 1980)

Books for older readers

Peter Chrisp, *Evacuation* (Mass-Observation Archive, University of Sussex Library, 1987)

B.S. Johnson, *The Evacuees* (Gollancz, 1968)

Peter Lewis, *A People's War* (Thames Television, 1986)

Robert Westall, *Children of the Blitz* (Penguin, 1985)

Ben Wicks, *No Time to Wave Goodbye* (Bloomsbury, 1988)

ACKNOWLEDGEMENTS

The publishers would like to thank the following for permitting us to quote from their sources. (The order of sources is as they appear in the text.) William Heinemann Ltd. for *France at War* by Somerset Maugham, 1940. Macmillan Publishers Ltd. for *The Week That France Fell* by Noel Barber, 1976. Lord Privy Seal's Office for *Evacuation Why and How?*, July 1939. Bloomsbury Publishing Ltd. for *No Time to Wave Goodbye* by Ben Wicks, 1988. Penguin Books Ltd. for *Children of the Blitz* by Robert Westall, 1985. Extracts from Mass-Observation copyright the Trustees of the Tom Harrisson Mass-Observation Archive, reproduced by permission of Curtis Brown Group Ltd. Thames Television for *A People's War* by Peter Lewis, 1986. The Women's Institute for *Town Children Through Country Eyes*. Hodder & Stoughton Ltd. for *The Cruellest Night* by Christopher Dobson, John Miller and Ronald Payne, 1979. Where sources have a name and location only, they were interviewed by the author.

The illustrations in this book were supplied by the following: E T Archives Limited 5(top); Imperial War Museum 5 (bottom), 7, 9, 15 (top), 20 (both), 22 (bottom), 24, 28, 29 (top); John Frost 13 (top); Mary Evans 15 (bottom); Peter Newark's Historical Pictures 25 (top); Popperfoto 10 (bottom), 12, 14, 16, 17 (top), 19 (top), 21, 22 (top), 27 (top); Topham *cover,* 6 (both), 8 (top), 10 (top), 11, 13 (bottom), 18, 19 (bottom), 23, 25 (bottom), 26, 27 (bottom); Wayland Picture Library 17 (bottom); Weimar Archive 8 (bottom), 29 (bottom). The artwork on page 4 is by Peter Bull Art Studio.

INDEX